THE RAMBLINGS OF AN AVERAGE JOE STOCK TRADER

By Christopher L. Boyer

Edition 1, 2011

I0463239

THE RAMBLINGS OF AN AVERAGE JOE STOCK TRADER

The average individual believes that investing in the stock market is just a gamble. They believe their hard earned dollars have the same odds of multiplying in the market, as they do on a casino craps table. The truth is the market is what you make it. You don't buy a house just by knowing its address. You investigate the area, drive the neighborhood, walk through the house, have it inspected, and have an appraisal done, all before you buy. In a lot of ways investing in the stock market is similar to investing in a piece of real estate. You can blindly buy a house, or you can do all you can to make sure your making a good investment in real estate. The more research and involvement you make in the market, the greater your risk/return ratio will be. Investing short-term or long-term in the market is the only action that I have found that provides you with the greatest opportunity of magnifying your current financial situation, with unlimited possibilities. Your financial future is only dependent upon your willingness to explore, learn, and experience the market.

Before you begin flipping pages you should know

THE DISCLAIMERS

This book is a composite of all the knowledge I have learned trading the market whether it was a positive experience or negative. I have tried to include all my experiences, so that you can learn from them. I had no one to teach me the ropes or there to hold my hand. For me it's all been a lot of trial and error reading books and asking questions of anyone that may have a slight idea of the market. You will find not many people in your immediate surroundings have a clue about the market. Unless you are fortunate you will find few people to talk to, and many will think your gambling. And as you advance in your quest for more knowledge about the market you will find fewer and fewer people to speak with. Try having a conversation with someone about Bollinger bands or inverted head and shoulder patterns.

In no way do I claim to know it all. I know that I am still learning. And it would be impossible for me to remember where all the information I have gathered inside my head, came from. So I say thank you to all those who have contributed to the construction and development of my neural pathways. At the end of this book I have listed a few of my favorite reads pertaining to the market, and why I felt those books were so beneficial to my success.

This book is written in a straight to the point format with stories, tips and ideas typed in a direct manner. You may find the order of information choppy and not flowing. My point in writing this book is not to become an expert writer. The point in this book is to help those out there learn just a little bit more about trading and investing. Many of the things in this book you will not find in other books. I am positive that there is at least one piece of information in this book that will cover the cost of buying it. I only wish someone would have told the contents of this book when I started out. This book would have saved me lots of time and thousands of dollars.

Sections of this book are written in a fashion that I only note topics you should learn, but I do not describe them to you. Example-- You should learn what a "wash sale" is.
These are areas you should do your own

research on. I am not spending the time to repeat what is best said somewhere else. I am not trying to write a repeat of other people's books, websites or lectures.

I use Scottrade as my online broker. The $7 online trades are decent, but compared to the other online brokers the amount of information that they give a beginner without additional fees (especially inactivity fees) more than pays for itself. Open an account if you just want up to the minute business news and interest paid on your checking account. Interest is minimal but probably better than the 0% you're getting now. One downfall that Scottrade has, or I don't understand, their advanced platform Scottrade Elite has a way to practice virtual trading. In order for you to have the Elite platform you must deposit $25,000 into the account. So you can't practice virtual trading unless you have money. So paper trade.

Times change, situations change, the market changes. The information contained in this book is my findings at the time I found them. You should always check with your financial advisor before making any type of investment decision or investment. Your financial advisor, accountant, banker, or brokerage office should have many articles pertaining to making investment choices.

This book is only a situational tip guide of my experiences.

This book is written based on east coast time. You should make adjustments to compensate for your time zone.

I do not work for and am in no way paid or sponsored by Scottrade. I have no affiliation with Scottrade other than being a customer myself. They have not paid me to promote their company and they make no claims as to the validity of any statements or to anything I write in this book pertaining to them.

Some of the information in this book may be simple to you. But not everyone starts in the same place. I find that sometimes the simple things are most easily forgotten.

Some interesting and fun things to do,

Get some highlighter pens. Highlight things you understand the first time you read this in one color. Mark the things you don't understand in another. As you start down Wall Street you may quickly realize you know nothing about the stock market, overall economy, investing and trading. As time passes and you continue your search for more knowledge come back and read this book again. Use another color highlighter. You will be amazed how much more you understand, agree with, and disagree with.

Watch a few stock movies. In six months watch those same stock movies. You will be amazed at what those people were talking about that you never realized before. A good one is the famous "Wall Street."

Try to find others that can begin this learning journey with you. Understanding the market is much easier if you have someone to learn with, and bounce ideas off of. If you wait to long to share with others you will find that your knowledge far exceeds theirs and you will spend most of your time just trying to explain the basics to them. Start a group or investment club. Stay away from online message boards. Message boards will cause you to panic out of, or into a trade. They can become a useful tool over time, but not for an inexperienced trader.

The beginning of my rambles,

I wish someone would have told me when I was 22 that trading the market was an option. No one I knew had any idea other than, "The stock market is gambling."

Depending on your level of investing you will be overwhelmed. DON'T PANIC. We all were at some point. This topic takes time to understand. Most K through 12 schools don't have general education programs in investing. In the beginning don't try to step out of the box. Don't try to come up with your own ideas, or formulate different strategies thinking you can do them all. You will only become bogged down. Your first step is to turn on CNBC at home, or if you have an XM radio tune it to CNBC while you're driving. Always have it playing in the background. You will be surprised at how much you will gradually pickup over time. Then start learning terminology. Many of the words used in investing are simple and just take a little time to add to your vocabulary. You don't want to get confused between bid and ask when you're trying to fill an order, that will cost you money. Then start learning some basic phrases and principles. Go to www.ivestopedia.com for tons of information, and once you open a brokerage account they will have lots of learning tools for you to take advantage of. Some people buy the "Idiots Guide," which is an ok place to start learning the basics, but you will quickly find out that all of the information can be found online and you just wasted 20 bucks.

Try doing this-- Watch the show fast money on CNBC. If you can watch that show from beginning to end and understand all the words, phrases and ideas that they are talking about (without pauses or hesitation) you then can start to develop your own investment style and can attempt riskier ideas or strategies.

If you're still working your day job, get a DVR so you can record the stock programs that you find most interesting or record CNBC during market hours. Then go back and compare the news to charts of how the market reacted during different parts of the day. I record Fast Money and Mad Money, on CNBC. Fast Money you will find has more short-term trading styles and the information is thrown out rather fast. Mad Money, with Jim Kramer, is a good learning tool that helps you understand basic ideas and principals. Both programs have up to date news, but I find Fast Money more useful. Remember Jim Kramer's comments can have a dramatic impact on your stock price, especially short-term.

Another fantastic place to go get a ton of information is http://daytradingradio.com. The host is just like the rest of us, just trying to make a dollar. He has hundreds of free web videos that help you understand the market and trading. You can also find them on www.youtube.com. The great thing about his site is each day the market is open he broadcasts all day over the internet. He also does some evening broadcasting too. Many of you will be trading alone, so his voice will quickly become your day trading partner. Check him out.

You can trade anything, stocks, options, futures, bonds, currency, and commodities. I choose stocks. That is what I trade and that is what this book is about. I could try trading the others but I don't know or understand the others, yet. Pick one thing and become great at it, which is what I have always been told. You will in time want to become more familiar with the others and how they influence your stocks. In time you will start to see the correlation one asset class, sector or industry plays on the other.

I try to stay away from penny stocks. And I believe most serious investors do. There is a reason there stock price is that price. You will understand more about pennies as you do your research. But for know I would recommend you stay away from stocks listed under $1.00.

Start looking to open an account with an online brokerage firm if you don't already have one. The reason why you should go ahead and start looking for a brokerage firm is the brokerage firm is going to have tutorials and research tools that will be extremely helpful as you learn. Also go ahead and make www.investopedia.com one of your favorite web pages. When you call your brokerage and ask a question if they don't immediately know the answer, this is the site they go to find it.

Choosing a brokerage.
I have already told you who I use. You can do your own research on the different types and advantages and disadvantages. It doesn't really matter what your commissions are as long as you're making money. Like in any business, try to keep your costs low, but don't stress to much (especially in the beginning) on what your paying for commissions. Stress more on understanding your downside risks in an investment.

Most online brokers don't let you test drive their full platform unless you open an account, deposit money, and make a certain number of trades. Scottrade gives you the most real time information on their basic platform that I have found that is the best place to start. You can open an account online as long as you have decent credit. They want you to deposit money and will call you a couple days after you open the account but they don't force you to deposit great amounts.

This book is not about who you should use as

a broker, or about choosing a broker. But, a few simple things to look for when choosing a broker are; no inactivity fees, low commissions for unlimited shares, free tutorial and educational programs, free streaming news, free streaming real-time stock quotes, software or programs to help keep track of your trades and compatible with your tax software.

It is all about the money.

Next you should know about not having enough money to trade. You might be starting out with $100 or $100,000. It doesn't matter. Right now you need to focus on understanding what it is your doing. No lie, it is a little difficult the less money you have. It takes more time and calculated moves to get the best rate of return with less money. It will be slow and slippery. The more you can begin with the easier it will be to turn a substantial profit or loss. Yes I said loss. The more you have does not mean you will be any better at trading. It just means you have the greater chance at loosing more. You should only begin with the amount that you are completely comfortable with loosing. You must always weigh your downside more heavily then your upside. You must always know your exit points to the downside before you calculate your exit points to the upside. You must never put a trade in place if you have not developed a plan. Plan your trade, and stick to your plan. This principal will save you more money and help protect your primary investment.

The overall point in this paragraph is just start learning. If you have .$1 or $100,000 it doesn't matter the quicker you start learning the easier trading will be when you do have more money. And once you see the awesome power of the market you will be driven to come up with more money. Don't borrow your grandmother's retirement money!

If you have more money you will be able to buy more shares. It's all about magnifying your returns while limiting your losses. You can buy 100 shares of XYZ for $1000 looking for a .04 move. Or you can buy 1000 shares of XYZ for $10,000 looking for that same .04 move. Your return on the 100 is $4(-10 after commissions). And your return on the 1000 shares is $40 (+$26 after commission). Same trading plan, just more money to buy more shares. Get comfortable with calculating larger numbers. Calculating larger numbers makes it easier to see the money as just numbers and helps lower your levels of fear.

Trading on margin. If you plan on making short term trades you want margin. Lots of books and web sites tell you margin is bad. But in reality you can not trade without it unless you have huge amounts of cash. The main reason you need it is;
If you buy a stock today, that purchase transaction takes 3 days to process. If you

decide to sell that purchase the same day, you have to wait 3 days for that transaction to clear. Your funds will not be available for 3 days. With margin your funds are made immediately available to you. So you can continue to make trades. Each trade ties up your immediate available cash. Without margin you will be limited to only trading the available cash in your account.

Like a credit card only use it when you need to use it. Don't max it out or you will find when something goes against you, your losses are magnified greatly. Be cautious. Oh yea, by the way carrying margin overnight costs money. Interest. But don't panic, with most accounts the interest is so low that 15000 in margin only has 40-90 dollars a month in interest. Check with your brokerage and get them to give you the exact calculations on determining your daily margin interest rate at different amounts borrowed. Make they show you how to calculate it. The guy or gal at the desks in the front probably won't be able to clearly tell you how. The office manager normally sits in the back corner. What I found is the margin interest is so minuet in comparison to money made that I could care less about it.

If you open your account with $2500 you only have $2500. If you open your account with $2500 and you have margin you have access to $5000. Wait it gets better. If you open your account with, or have a balance of $25,000 and you have margin you have access to $50,000. If you open your account with or have a balance of $25,000 and have margin and get classified as a pattern day trader you now have access too.........drum roll please.......$100,000. Yes 4 times the amount of what your account cash value is. So if you have a cash value of $32,560 and you have margin, and you are classified as a pattern day trader you have access to $130,240. The trick is if you use your DTBP (day trading buying power) you must have 50% of your account value closed out by the end of the day. The business day is not when the market closes at 4 pm. The day ends at the end of the after hours trading at 7:59 pm.

Now go open your account.

Familiarize yourself with their website or platform. Watch all the tutorials and web casts. Now watch them again and take notes. The more you are familiar with their site the easier it will be to find information when you really need it.

Practice making charts and pulling up information. Change the time frames. Read the different charting tools. Familiarize yourself with opening multiple windows and charts.

Learn about trend lines, channels, and support and resistance lines. Practice drawing all on charts. This is something that will take time and practice. Find videos online showing you how and where they should be drawn.

Go out and get this book. "Short-term Trading in the New Stock Market," written by Toni Turner.
The first half of this book is taught as if you are a student in a class, and the second half is written in a more advanced style. This is the best book on the market to learn the bones of what you need to learn.
Note**I read the sections on "TRIC and TRIN" and I did not find those indicators useful or easy to set up, or follow. There is a section mentioning S&P Minis. Most of you probably don't have immediate access to this. Don't worry go to www.daytradingradio.com and he has it up on his web page most of the time. Watch his free web videos to

understand this more.

The meat of this book starts here. I am not going to repeat what you will find in other books for the most part. This is a lot of information. It is what I have experienced. Get comfortable we are now going to get choppy. Real choppy. The topics are going to bounce from phrase to phrase, but phrase has a meaning.

Two types of investors, technical and fundamental. You have probably heard all about fundamental and technical investors. The main thing you should realize is that fundamental investing is more long-term investing and technical investing is more short-term. Some people classify themselves into one or the other. Who cares? You should use what ever information you have available to you to make your investment decision. Don't get hung up on types. If your trading short-term and most short-term traders use technical, then you should also probably go with that approach.

There are only two things that drive the market. Fear and greed. That's it. You will realize that you are holding a stock too long out of fear or greed. You will realize you are not trading your plan out of fear or greed. You will lose money to fear and greed. You are going to have a constant battle with fear and greed. Learn to control fear and greed. Read books on controlling emotion.

Go ahead and pick 5 stocks. Any stocks just pick them. Put them on your watch list. Some people find it easy to pick stocks that you may be familiar with or use every day.

You can spend a lot of time just trying to learn what everything is, or you can understand what you need to know.

Words to learn; bid, ask, last, spread and volume.

Use paper trading in the beginning. Though real money has an emotion tied to it.

In the beginning try to watch stocks that are frequently mentioned in the news. This is a good way to learn company's tickers and familiarize you with different sectors, and industries. Watching these types of stocks will give you the opportunity to see how the media influences stock price. When an analyst mentions a stock punch it up on your screen and watch how the market moves the stock price in a direction. Jim Kramer, MAD MONEY, really can move a stock price.

Especially in after hours. Take notes while you watch programs and web videos. You will quickly realize there is an abundance of information for you to absorb. The hardest part you have to deal with is…drum roll please…knowing that you don't need to know everything. Most of the information written in books an on TV will not pertain to your trading style. Most information you hear on TV will just be a repeat of an earlier breaking news story. In time you will begin to filter out what is and is not important. Many repetitive events move the overall market. Get a large calendar and start writing down dates that certain events occur. Write down what type of influence it had on the market. Gradually do this over time. As months and years pass you will see the patterns. Remember in the beginning it will seem like sensory overload. You will not know what is important and what is not. Trading comes in time. The rhythm of the market reveals itself only in time. You will feel the market move. Your instincts will guide you. (But not hope)

The library. Many big name books about investing can be found at your local library for free. Great reads especially if they are already underlined. Don't be afraid to look

at the older books. Especially the real old
ones. Remember history repeats itself.
Always look at the copyright date to get an
idea of the mindset of the individual or
individuals writing the book. Think about
the state of the economy during that time
period. Be aware that older books have stock
prices in fractions, not decimals.

Go to www.daytradingradio.com and watch
all the videos. Oldest to newest in that order.
I think there is 300 or so. This is a great
place to go to visually learn, and have things
explained in a clear easy to understand
manner. I wish I would have had this site to
go to when I first started out. And I admit
when I watched his videos the first time I
learned a bunch. Each time I view them
something else stands out. Check it out.
I am not being compensated by the site and I
have no affiliation with the site. I actually
have never met the host. But I do owe him
many thanks for all he does for all us
investors and traders!

The stock market does not have to go up for
you to make money. You just need the
market to move.

This next concept will be difficult to grasp in

the beginning especially if you are new to trading, but I choose to mention it now so that you can understand the previous statement, and the different variations in trading. If you develop a plan to trade a stock long for a particular catalyst, you should also know that you can trade the stock the opposite of your plan.

Selling short. Selling shares you don't own at a price, in an effort to buy the shares back at a lower price, capturing the difference. Why is selling short is scary? The pitfalls of selling short while not owning the stock long are, you have the potential of losing everything and then some. Do more research on short selling, if this is a type of investing that interests you.
Here is a short story about how one could use shorting to their advantage-
There was a guy that was a professional short seller. He heard that a company was manufacturing clothes made out of a certain percentage of seaweed. He bought the clothes sent them to an independent lab only to find out that there was no seaweed or very little. He aggressively sold the company short and then released his findings to the media. The stock quickly dropped. He quickly covered his short for a nice profit.

Those that shorted for the long run are paying the price. Type in "short selling seaweed clothing" in the Google search engine you will find the story.

The 25000 dollar rule! You can only make 4 same day trades in a 5 open business day period. A same day trade is- if you buy a stock today and sell the same stock today that's a same day trade. Do more research on types of same day trades. If you make more than four same day trades in a five day period you will be classified as a pattern day trader and the government requires you to have $25,000 in you account. Don't worry about why, you just need to know that is the way it is. If you make more than four and you don't have the 25 thousand needed you will get a call. They will warn you the first time after they give you the speech about day trading. Your next options will be 1) come up with $25,000 or 2) don't do it again.
The penalty for making more trades without enough money is removal of your margin. You will understand more about using margin and its benefits/pitfalls later. You just need to know that you don't want to loose margin for now. (Consult your broker for more info pertaining to the $25,000 rule) One easy way around the rule is to short the

same number of shares you own. Then cover both the next day. You will however pay double the commissions when it's over. For example. I buy 1000 shares of XYZ. It runs up a few minutes later creating a nice profit. You know you can't sell the shares without using a same day trade, so you short 1000 shares of the same stock. Locking in the profit. You pay commissions to buy the stock, sell the stock, short the stock and then buy the short back. You will understand in time.

Be aware that not all stocks have shares available to short.

Another way to compensate for limited trading is time your trades perfectly. Save your same day trades for a major crisis moment when you have to get out fast. In the beginning I would sit, watch and wait for the perfect setup. And I would have planned my exit for the next day at an exact time or condition. This was very time consuming and yielded only a small gain. Overtime I realized you can't call the exact top or the exact bottom. There are signs to indicate a top or bottom is near and we will discuss some of them later in this book.

Remember every investor/trader is different.

Their trading ideas and timelines are different then yours. What I think is a great deal may only be a great deal for the next thirty seconds or two days. If I don't tell you more details like, the time frame or the amount of move I am looking for, my great deal could be your loss.

Tax and the day trader. I am not an accountant. So talk to and hire a tax accountant.

Look up information on a "wash sale." You will find that this topic is tricky.

Look up information on where to place stops and stop limits. Though when extremely short-term trading you will not have enough time to place stops. Always plan your trade, and stick to your plan.
Stops only work during market hours. 9 am till 4 pm. They will not get you out of a position in pre market and after market hours.

In after hours trading--If you try to place a trade on your order entry window and it doesn't fill rather quickly, check and make sure you marked after hours trade in the correct box.
THANKS ROBERT FOR THAT ONE!

Finding the market rhythm. You'll know it when…you are in it. Sit and play with the market everyday from open till close, eventually you will be able to feel the pulse of the market. In those times you will make your best and most profitable trades.

Catalyst- A catalyst is an event that may occur that will directly cause the stock price to rise or fall. It could be an earnings report or a major news announcement. It could also be as simple as a famous investor mentioning the stock at 3:30 pm during an interview. If you know prior to the interview that the investor will be mentioning the stock whether positively or negatively that small mention could be enough to move the stock the ten cents you were looking for. Remember 10 cents on 10000 shares is 1000 dollars.

10000 share trades are called block shares. When watching the time and sales window if you see block shares trading that usually means larger fish are in the pond. Likewise if you see lots of small odd shares trading (ex. 154, 74, 56, 213) you should know that small fish are selling or buying. This could be an indication of the direction of the stock

I worked in a convenience store and had the opportunity to get newspapers right when they came in during third shift. Business was slow so I had the opportunity to read all the major papers including the local ones. What I realized is newspapers are an abbreviated version of the past. But by reading it first you are normally ahead of those that don't read them. Remember newspapers are old news. The internet provides almost real time breaking news for free. Don't get caught up in specialty newspapers that are a collection of computer generated charts, instructions on how to read the charts, and a few articles. You will find that is a waste of money.

The market can be traded from 8 am eastern to 8 pm eastern.
8 am till 9:30 is the pre-market. 4:00 pm till 8 pm is the after market. You should now that most online brokers do not allow you to trade from 9:15 am till 9:30 am, and from 4:00 pm till 4:15 pm. And what is most important about these times is… this is when the big news that moves stock prices normally comes out. Example-- So if you are in a trade and the earnings come out after the bell it most likely will come out at between 4:00 and 4:15. You will not be able to exit your position. But other people will be able

to exit theirs, driving the stock price in one direction or the other. Two ways to protect yourself from drastic after hours moves is 1)either go flat each day and carry nothing overnight or 2)short an equal number of shares as your long position.

Look up more information on Level II. This is normally only available on advanced platforms and normally will cost a fee if you don't make a certain number of trades per month. During market hours it is a helpful tool but I find it especially helpful in pre-market and after hours. Trading without Level II in pre-market and after market hours is like trying to trade with one eye closed. Level II is also the only way I know how to spot the axe. Do more research on the "axe." I have only positively found the axe a couple handfuls of times. It is extremely profitable to find the axe, though extremely difficult to find more information on.

There are many daily events that occur at approximately the same time every day. In the book "Short-Term Trading in the New Stock Market," written by Toni Turner, you will find a list of all the days occurrences with times. The market does move or calm down at those approximate times. One time you want to add to that chart is around 3:52 pm. Approximately around 3:52 pm, what ever the market is doing watch for it to reverse. The reason for this appears to be that so many people that went long (or short) that day want to close their positions. In order to do that they must do the opposite. Sell if long, or buy if short.

Pay attention to weekends and holidays. People don't like to hold stocks over longer periods of time.

Pay attention to historical events. Terrorists like to attack on historical days. A terrorist attack will have a dramatic downward effect on the market.

Buy or check out at the library "Day Traders Almanac. " It is very interesting to read. You will understand why when you get one.

Penny stocks. Companies are worth pennies for a reason.

If you want to know how a business is doing (especially retail) go hang out in the store. Remember the research you're doing is only regional.

Know the difference between a short-term trade time frame, and a long-term trade time frame.

Patterns. Why patterns happen. If you have 100 people all doing the same thing at the same time when a certain event occurs that creates a pattern. If it occurs enough times then it becomes a predictable pattern. Patterns occur all day long, every day, every month, every year.

Search for patterns on the 6 month daily chart. This is where you will find most patterns.
The longer the pattern is in time the more reliable it is as an indicator.
Don't try real hard to make something out of nothing. The pattern you are looking for will be pretty obvious.

The 5 main indicators I use are 1) Stochastic 2) moving averages 3) trendlines 4) chart patterns 5) support and resistance lines. I wait for 3 or more of these to set up prior to making a trade.

Setting your charts and screens up to look like every one else. What you want to do is be able to recognize the patterns that others create. If all the charts on your screen match that of all the other full time investors at the big brokerage firms you have a small window into their minds. You want your chart type, moving average lines, bands and time frames to be that most similar to the overall masses. I have been working on this for many years.

So far my current setup is as follows.

I use two screens, sometimes three. You will realize that all the information that you want to see doesn't fit on just one. And remember the bigger the screens the better.

For short term trades

Set up 3 charts (at least)

One chart should be on a 5 minute time scale

One chart should be on a 10 minute time scale

One chart should be on a 60 minute time scale

Use candlestick charts, with simple moving averages (SMA).

SMA=10

SMA=21

SMA=50

SMA=100

SMA=200

Add SMA to all your charts.

Stochastic (14, 3, 3) -- Overbought and oversold indicator.

Bollinger Bands-out side the bands are overbought and over sold indicators. Volume-See the volume indicator as a lie detector. The higher the volume the more truthful and reliable the move is. Example- If you have a stock price shoot up on low volume the odds of the stock holding the higher price is low.

Also have charts set up for S&P500, NASDAQ, and Dow. It really just depends on the stock you have. It the stock you are trading is in the NASDAQ have a NASDAQ chart up.

The S&P500 index is the most widely used and traded index.

Learn about the NASDAQ futures and S&P500 futures. Pay special attention to what they mean. Don't be surprised to find yourself getting up in the middle of the night to check them.

Learn about the VIX. (CBOE volatility index) Patterns are not predictable in the market if the VIX is trading above about 32. Be cautious. Times change.

Buying your first stock is like standing in line

for a roller coaster ride. When you have finally made the purchase you are riding the ride. You will understand this immediately once you place your first trade.

Pulling the trigger. Practice a few times pulling up an order entry window. Fill it out completely. Then slowly move the cursor over the input order button. Do you feel your heart beginning to race? This is real money. This is a real trade. You need to get comfortable with pulling the trigger. Stick to your plan and take action.

Knowing when to walk away. There are many stocks to choose from. Don't get stuck trying to get back to even in the same stock. Each trade is different. If your initial plan failed, learn from your mistake and move on. If each time I said to myself maybe I am not cut out for this, I stopped trading I would have never became better.

When listening to someone talk about an investment being good or bad always pay attention to the time frame they are talking about. If I say XYZ is good to buy, what good is that information? If I say XYZ is good to buy today and I am going to hold it to this price or this day, what good is that

information. Always pay attention. You will
find that most investors/analysts on TV don't
announce time frames often. They make
generalized statements never really locking
anything down to anything. Pay attention.

CNBC and what is meant by breaking news.
Breaking news moves a stock price whether
it is a lot or a little, but be careful. You could
have breaking news that comes out at 6:05
am for the first time but all day long they
announce the news as BREAKING each time
they report it. Make sure if they say breaking
that it is actually breaking news, meaning it
literally just came out.

MAD Money, Jim Kramer can have the
opposite effect on a stock. He can kill a
really good set up.

If Jim Kramer, comes on TV around mid day
and mentions that he is doing a segment on a
certain stock later that day on his show, pay
close attention to if he says it in a positive or
negative manor. If he pumps a stock on his
show it normally has an immediate affect on
the stock price in after hours. Easy way to
make money.

Fast Money. The closest you will get to real

time traders sharing their opinions daily. On their web site they have an interesting section called Trade School. Watch those videos.

Create weekly stock watch lists. Each weekend I spend time going through every chart in the S&P500 looking for setups/patterns. It took me a long time to set this up but it was worth the effort. I know there are stock screeners that will do this for me, but I like the being involved. "Trade Ideas" is a program that has numerous settings to find any stock in pretty much any situation. Scottrade provides this as part of their Elite platform for no cost.

Before you short a stock always check the ex-dividend date. Don't short if you will be holding through this date or you could be out of a lot of money. Learn more about this.

Quarterly earnings dates. Magical moments that occur. Go to a site that gives you a list of the quarterly earnings dates. Yahoo finance or CNBC are good. Go through each date and make a list of all stocks you are familiar with or are currently trading or watching. In the beginning you will not recognize many, but don't worry in time you will find many familiar. As the dates approach observe how the market moves the stock price. Watch for patterns that occur. In time as each quarter passes of you doing this you will start to see larger patterns and feel the market push and pull. Different stocks respond differently at different times of the year. Over time you will be able to notice unique movements, such as XYZ runs up into earnings or release dates, then sells off drastically. The sooner you get started doing this the sooner you will be more in the rhythm of the market.

Stand clear when the president speaks. The market will typically sell off going into a presidential speech during business hours. Be cautious. After the market realizes the president isn't saying anything that directly affects the market, it will gradually recover.

Big company stocks in sectors influence all stocks in that sector. If you notice your stock is going down even though it just announced fantastic news or was upgraded be cautious. Look at the overall sector that the stock trades in. Maybe another giant company just released bad news. Use this as a buying opportunity if the news only directly affects the one company.

If a company reports unbelievable earnings and raises forward guidance beyond what was expected, pay attention. Find out what companies do business, or provide goods to that company. Pay close attention to their up coming earnings. Watch how those stocks move on this news. Those companies may be good short term investments.

Hope is never a word you should use. If you are hoping your stock is going up or going to rebound, exit it. You should never invest on hope.

Whole numbers. People buy and sell normally at whole numbers. If a stock is at $9.87 pay special attention as it approaches $10. If you start to see heavy selling pressure it may be a sign of a short term reversal. Whole numbers are 1, 2, 3, 4, 5, 6, etc. but not 1.22 or 5.67. Another example; pick the whole number out of this line up 56.96, 56.97, 56.98, 56.99, 57.00, 57.01, 57.02. If you said 57.00 your right.

If everyone has already bought the stock who is left to buy it. Which direction do you think the price will move?

If everyone has already sold the stock who is

left to sell it. Which direction do you think the price will move?

Double bottom formations are bullish. The saying is "there is no such thing as a triple bottom." Learn about double bottom formations.

With channels-- Wait for three tests of the upper and lower trend lines, then look for the stock to setup and an entry point.

If a stock trades down on good news it may be at a top.

If a stock doesn't go lower on bad news it may be at a bottom.

With a head and shoulders pattern (or inverted head and shoulders pattern) look for the heaviest volume on the head area of the chart. The left and right shoulder volume should also be heavier.

Look for downward slopping channels off a recent high. The more it pulls back the greater the chance of a breakout to the upside.

Learn about "measured moves." Measured

moves give you an indication of how much a stock price will potentially move after a breakout.

Very important. All gaps close. Look up gap trading. Typically five to seven days after a stock gaps be prepared for it to close the gap. Make sure you pay close attention to the volume. Remember volume is a truth indicator.

Learn about dividend paying companies and learn about their ex-divided date. This technique can be a steady stream of income month to month.

Never add money to a losing position. A losing position is when a stock has gone against you beyond your original exit price. This is different from dollar cost averaging. Learn more about dollar cost averaging.

People go on vacation in the summer months, so plan on lower volume levels. I believe the phrase is "Sell in May and go away."

Bull market- 3 days up 2 days down.

Bear market- 3 days down 2 days up.

September and October are normally negative months, so be cautious. Except during election years.

November sell off- Large investment companies will exit positions 30 days prior to end of year so they can reenter those same positions in January. Tax Reasons.

Yahoo Finance is a great source of information but stay away from the message boards. Many hack traders start rumors and tell lies to try to influence their stock. These rumors become unwanted truths and could panic you out of a trade. Create your plan. Trade your plan. Stick to your plan.

Level II allows you to see the buyers and sellers of a particular stock all lined up. Learn more about Level II.

Buy the rumor, sell the news.

Overseas markets influence the futures.

The power of owning multiple shares;
1 share up $.01= $.01 gain
100 shares up $.01= $1.00 gain
1,000 shares up $.01= $10.00 gain
10,000 shares up $.01= $100.00 gain

Note** the more shares you own in a position the longer it may take for you to exit that position.

The "All or none" option on your order entry window. Use it wisely. If you need to get out of your position fast this box could prevent you from doing so. Learn more about "all or none" "AON"

What type of person is the person you are listening to?
If the person you are listening to trades on a monthly time frame their stock charts are set up that way. If the person you are listening to is a day trader their setups will be on shorter chart time frames like intraday or daily. Always pay attention to the speaker's trade time frame or style of trade. Kramer appears to be monthly to yearly. Fast Money appears to be intraday or weekly. Remember the majority of the big players are monthly to annually.

Scale into positions you are uncomfortable with.

You always hear diversify, diversify, and diversify. Well I will tell you to try to diversify with $100 dollars or even $1000 dollars. It is not easy to diversify and still yield a nice return. Be cautious. The truth is it is really hard to diversify with little money. I did not start diversifying till I got around $10,000 dollars. And even at that point it is very limiting.

Learn about the "short float."

Learn about a "short squeeze."

Trade the trend. Never go against the overall trend. Especially in the beginning.

The more a stock is mentioned in the news the more the stock could move.

Learn about buy put options to protect your downside risk on your long positions. Buying a put is like buying insurance on your car. This can save you money if you're waiting for a future catalyst.

The Dow and S&P are lagging indicators.

NASDAQ stocks have more transparency. (Level II)

Dow and S&P have longer trading patterns

because they have longer institutional investors.

If you are starting out with less than $25,000 do more research on trading S&P mini futures. You can trade these without being classified as a pattern day trader.

The VIC is a measure of fear in greed in the market. It is based on option pricing. Market goes up the VIC goes down. Market goes down the VIC goes up. You can trade the VIC with the ticker VXX. But be cautious they do not move equally.

Learn about Stochastic, an over bought and over sold indicator. Watch the free videos on www.daytradingradio.com he has some great videos on stochastic and why to use them. Under 20 oversold. Over 80 overbought.

Learn about candlestick charts and why the stock price may reverse after 3 to 4 same color bars.

Learn about the "Inverted head and shoulders pattern." This is the one that has the potential to make you some good money.

Always keep a log of your trades. It's an

annoying pain at first but you will eventually get used to it. It is the best way to learn from your mistakes.

Some people only trade in the morning and at the close. This style can be very profitable.

Exercise daily. It is a great way to relieve stress.

Look for big stock price moves around the 200 day moving average line.

"This profession demands you to have patients, discipline and do a lot of hard work." www.daytradingradio.com

You don't always have to be in the market. Wait for the market to show you an entry point. If you are itching to be in the market, walk away or just buy a small amount of shares to get your fix.

Always check with your financial advisor, and tax attorney prior to making any investment decisions.

Last but not least, trading is the most mentally challenging thing I have ever done. Every moment of every day is a new and exciting challenge that is not easily compared to any other endeavor that you will try. But if successful, you have the opportunity to be the wealthiest person ever.

Recommended readings;
Stock Traders Almanac, Yale and Jeffery
Hirsh.
The Psychology of Trading, Brett
Steenbarger Ph. D.
Japanese Candlestick Charting Techniques,
Steve Nison
Beyond Candlesticks: More Japanese
Charting Techniques Revealed, Steve Nison.
Short-Term Trading in the New Stock
Market, Toni Turner
A Beginners Guide to Day Trading, Toni
Turner
Getting Started in Chart Patterns, Thomas N.
Bulkowski

Recommended sites;
www.daytradingradio.com
www.yahoofinance.com
www.cnbc.com
www.investopedia.com
www.fool.com
www.bloomberg.com
www.dividend.com
www.youtube.com
www.scottrade.com

Published by Christopher L. Boyer
January 2011